THE LEADINC

Roger Elk

Roger Elkin

The High Window

First published in the UK in 2020 by The High Window Press
3 Grovely Close
Peatmoor
Swindon
SN5 5DN
Email: abbeygatebooks@yahoo.co.uk

Designed and typeset in Palatino Linotype
by The High Window Press.
Cover artwork: 'Where Now?' © Erica Brooke, has been made
available by kind permission of Jackie and Bob Foster.
Printed and bound by kdp.amazoncom

For Eileen

who feeds my hunger with food for thought - always

"It is vain to hope for any permanent and extensive advantage from any system of emigration which does not primarily apply to Ireland, whose population, unless some other outlet be opened to them, must shortly fill up every vacuum created in England or Scotland, and to reduce the labouring classes to a uniform state of degradation."

Revd. Thomas Robert Malthus,
An Essay on the Principle of Population, 1798

"History," Stephen said, "is a nightmare from which I am trying to awake."

James Joyce, *Ulysses*, 1922

"The basic project of art is always to make the world whole and comprehensible, to restore it to us in all its glory and its occasional nastiness, not through argument but through feeling, and then to close the gap between you and everything that is not you, and in this way pass from feeling to meaning. It's not something that committees can do. It's not a task achieved by groups or by movements. It's done by individuals, each person mediating in some way between a sense of history and an experience of the world."

Robert Hughes, *The Shock of the New*, 1991

Contents

Holding

this potato, flat in the hand,
its shape filling the palm-bowl,
fully: rounded, smooth pebble-like;

clutching this, firm in the hand,
its smooth curves fitting the curve
of skin between palm and fingers;

bending fingers and thumb, curving
over its smooth skin; the whole stone
of it lying flat, weighty, comfortable

becomes flint tool, to use, clutched,
and cutting: at ground, at land, at twig, at wood,
at limb, stripping flesh from vein, from bone:

handled so, kindles an atavistic ritual:
the bond between stone and curving hand
bound up in the rhythm of living:

earth   stone   bone   history

and the curve holding it all together

the holding of this potato.

"Nearly a stone of the root was taken into the stomach of the Irish labourer per diem."
W.R. Wilde, **The Food of the Irish**, *Dublin University Magazine, 1854, xl111, page 131*

Statue Group, Custom House Quay, Dublin
Famine by Rowan Gillespie, unveiled October 1998

Strokestown? Youls be needing the N4, N5.
So it's right at the mini-bout. Straight down
to the traffic-lights. And the next. Then, it's left
over the Liffey, and right again at the lights.
As easy as breathing. Yous can't miss it.

We nudge, bumper to bumper, through the first lights,
our eyes panning all sides as we take in the city sights,
until our glance - pulled without our knowing - locks
on a memorial-sculpture grouped by the quayside.

Some remnant of education dredged from memory
means we guess their significance before we've had chance
to reckon them: seven figures – men, women, children –
not bundled in huddling pity like Rodin's *Burghers of Calais*
but islanded in sad detachment, larger than life
and cast in burnished bronze: such beauty among such loss.

Tall and straight-spined they have that quiet dignity
we've seen in news-footage of Ethiopian famine victims:
hollow eyes, sunk cheeks, drawn looks, and skeletal the brows,
the frame, the whole form elongated - (similarities exist
in period illustrations where suffering's been distilled to Art) –
and around them an aura of silence, almost tangible, as if
aware their beseeching speech won't alter a thing,
they've fallen to silent keening that takes all breath away.

Turning backs on Ireland and the soil that has worn them
sickle-thin to betrayal, and with eyes glazed in resignation,
they gaze beyond the Liffey's mouth, Dublin harbour, and on,

Eastward, out, to England and the unknown. Between them
is everything they own, held in baskets and panniers:
a lifetime reduced to bundles; themselves standing-rags, leaving
behind barren fields and poverty's despair for a new life.

Quick. Camera. Quick.

But our fumbling is useless: the lights change; and the weight
of traffic pushes us across Talbot Memorial Bridge; then it's right
at the lights, and west along Liffey's south bank, all the time
keeping watch for the N4, and the road-fork to the N5
just beyond *Mother Hubbard's* trucking-stop.

           Sniggering at this mix of myth and Irish wit,
we cannot help our questionings. Given what we've seen in Art,
what use in letting History put its special slant on truth?
What cost?

"Art is not truth. It is a lie that makes us realise the truth." Pablo Picasso

Journeying

I   Driving west into the diving sun, its honeyed haze
glazing the late April hedgerows from behind,
and tipping the hawthorns - gold on white and green.

Almost Elysian the fields in this twilight,
the last slanting rays flooding the rolling oceans
of meadow with vistas of pastureland broken only
by odd copses dotted towards changing skylines
and slices of bright sunlight on distant loughs.

No tillage to be seen as we speed through town
and village: but land given over to grazing,
with cattle, faint temple-etchings against light,
trundling their hulks – heavy and full – and straggling
beside blackthorns, or huddled, squatting in hollows;
and sheep with their haunted madman looks – so many.

And nowhere the earth upturned in fields,
apart from sheep-tracks and cattle scrums at gateways.
But earth upturned – courtesy of Europe – for roadworks,
building-sites, marinas: a fresh prosperity setting handprints
on the land, as roads assert impatience
in by-pass and carriageway; and townships expand
in an arrogance that mocks Oxfam posters, like those
at Longford's roadside with grim, skeletal figures carrying
that special brand of handsomeness that famine emanates
and underwritten by legends begging charity:

I'm not hungry for advancement; I'm just hungry.

II   As if in on cue, the land collapses from abundance to scrub
with rough patches hanging on to ancient patternings:
tracts of abandoned grassland, boggy with cotton-grass and sedge;
grave-shapes where, decades past, space was staked out for earth-
turf, the sunken beds like coffins cleaved out of peat; low stone-
walling, broken down and holding nothing in; coarse gorse
yellowing at the field-edge; the tumbled frames of barns
 and small farms, families long gone.

III   Suddenly, the patterns of husbandry resume
in what seems a renewed rhythm, field after field, counterpointing
the road: the grazing cattle at pasture, grass nudging to lushness,
vast plateaus of greenness – a sense of plenty stretching beyond.

And, sooner than expected, we've arrived:
a nothing sort of place with its string
of nondescript grey buildings relieved from facelessness
by occasional pebble-dash and lime-wash;
the tree-lined mall with its strange litter of ravens
tumbling from rooftops like slates;
and the archetypal Irish rigmarole:
Guinness signs, the bars, the local Spar, Bank of Ireland –
so much the stuff of jokes: *Blink, and you'll miss it.*
So there seems nothing much to make us stay,
till our eyes light on the tourist signs:

> *Strokestown Park House and Gardens*
> *Carvery and Famine Museum –*
> *a full day's entertainment*

and faces grimace with this final irony.

Stable Truths: The Irish National Famine Museum

From outside, this block of Georgian elegance -
its broad wooden gates, arch-shaped and spaced
at regular intervals in perfect symmetry along the inner face
of the brick-built south-wing elevation - celebrates
dignity, purpose and proportion: an arranged compactness
somehow reducing scale and making everything manageable.

Inside, where sight adjusts to a different light as subtly elusive
as dusk, dimensions alter, and walls seem taller, wider, broader.
What impresses, first, is their massiness: seven feet thick;
then next, it's the rhythm of the building: those eleven sections
of vaulted ceilings groined like elaborate monastic cloisters
or some Romanesque cathedral. Overawed, we double-check.
Surely this isn't some fantastic joke: all these Tuscan columns,
this spread of wealth just to shelter the Mahon teams of horse?

Exploring deeper, there's more to set us wondering,
as the stable-space gives way to ordered displays
with exhibits, pictures, models, maps, plans, cartoons,
that measure History's relentless tread.

Does the selecting act, *per se*, compromise objectivity?
Can History ever be free from bias? What makes fact
no more than that: just fact, pure and simple?

And what of words? What ironies
lie behind the use of such prescriptive terms as
       "conacre", "cottier", "clachan",
        "booleying", "spalpeens", and "lumper"?

Does their unfamiliarity excuse our wider ignorance?
Can absence of emotion hamper meaning?

Or are these just other forms of proportion serving further
purposes by reducing truth to nothing more
than a matter of semantics?

And do words betray where silences deceive?

"The house's former stables, marvellously vaulted buildings in their own right, house an often chilling
and ever stimulating museum detailing the Famine's effects upon the Mahon's tenants and its wider
impact."   Paul Gray & Geoff Wallis, **The Rough Guide to Ireland**, (2008), page 500

Conacre

Was how over a third of the population –
cottiers and the landless agricultural poor –
managed for decades to stave off starvation
by living on as little as one eighth of an acre
and borrowed time.

Was where, by verbal agreement and public bidding –
nothing more formal, legal or binding –
contracts were made with middlemen-agents
that gave licence to occupy those slips of earth
(sniggers, rood-land, stang, score- and quarter-ground)
for one growing season's tillage.

Was when permission was given
to build windowless cabins paid for
against agreed amounts of days' labour,
the rest of the rent (sometimes twice the price
of leased land so high the demand)
to be paid after harvesting. With luck.

Was what drove landowners to ready the land
by spreading manure; while the cottier provided
seed, and planted, tended, garnered his single crop –
mostly potatoes. If harvest was good, had stuff
to barter; if failed, then cabin and contents -
everything, and more - were lost.

Was why, between '45 and '50,
as lumper crops festered and rotted,
and small-holdings consolidated to over 15 acres,

and grazing replaced tillage,
these two million landless poor
gradually vanished through death and emigration.

Was how, where, when, what, and why
"conacre" joined "spalpeen" and "lumper",
"cottier" and "booleying"
to become little more than footnotes
in Ireland's history-books.

"The whole business was a speculation in food itself, for if the conacre failed the only escape from starvation was begging on the roads. The landlord ... had no hope of recovering the promised rent in the event of the failure of the crop. Conacre provided the labouring classes with food independently of the fluctuating markets. By furnishing a ready source of food supply, it undoubtedly encouraged subdivision, early marriage, and large families." E.R.R. Green, **The Great Famine**, (1956), page 95

Booleying

May 1st, day of changes, when cattle
were released from wintering byres
back into out-fields to lush Spring growth.

Then it was drovers were chosen
from clachan-lads for taking heifers and stirks
to summer mountain pastures,
and when booley-folds were reached down from rafters,
their snagged blackthorn-laths and willow-sticks replaced
and everything readied for the creaghting –
cattle jostling thin flanks in their rhythmic–river's
slow progress through dust and mud;
past turbary-stacks of fire-turf sliced from bogland;
along hedgerows, hawthorns crimson-tipping into leaf;
beside drystone walls; through sloping fields pocked
with ladysmock and buttercup; over cotton-bog and sedge,
the bracken-crooks; through sulphur maze of gorse –
all the time climbing, slow, steady –
cattle splatting, and low mooing - up,
out to the high wild Curlew hills
and the freedom fields of summer pasturing.

Once there, shieling-bivouacs settled with bracken for shelter,
willow-sticks firmed, booley-folds opened, the cattle ambled freely,
sharing wide views with the larks, with below them
clachan-villages reduced to nothings in the clear summer light,
the conacre lazy-beds changing from earth-browns
to greens over the weeks, and, beyond, the Connaught plain
spread out chalice-like, its loughs and rivers glinting
in slicing sunlight or shrouded by rain-cloud
louring from the west.

And, at dusk, this unleased plenty safe-havened,
with cattle held secure all through till September,
under the evening luminosity after rain, or dull-bloodied sunsets,
and long nights under the stars, the wide skies

and then the return descent,
to turf-warmth and peat-reek, the measured existence
of wintering dark.

"*The system of booleying… The young people went up with cattle on the mountains for the summer months.*" E.E.R. Green, **The Great Famine: Grazing and Dairy-Farming**, (1956), page 114

Spalpeens

Framed by their labour –
their Gaelic name translates as "penny scythes" –
this surplus underclass, poorest of the poor,
didn't even have the means to squeeze out
the half-acre rent their cottier-neighbours could:
a scythe was almost all they had.

Victims of evicting middlemen,
they outlawed themselves in mountain glens,
the blue-misted hills, the heath-thickets, and brown peat-bogs –
sparse habitats that matched their poverty -
where they dragged their families up:
living to thinness, sleeping rough in ditches,
or holed-up in sod-huts and caves, in briar-bush-clumps
with cast-off sacking for door-hanging and bracken for roofs –
not even the Bantu luxury of corrugated tin –
or beneath tree-roots.

Theirs was a feral existence, till emerging in late Spring,
they descended, shy-eyed and other-suspicious,
their scythes wrapped in rags over shoulders,
to meadowlands, for casual labour, blade against blade –
a penny a day: swish, swish - the cut of sweeping steel
from July through to September, and – swish, swish –
swaths of grass, of wheat, of corn lay shorn before them,
when time to move back to the conacre-plots
and the second potato-crop.

Was they that migrated annually -
nearly sixty thousand listed in the '41 Census -
passing through the ports, and back again,
of Dublin, Drogheda and Cork, Liverpool and Bristol,
for summer harvesting, and bringing to England

their animal stink, their lice, their smoke-grimed skin,
their drink, their Gaelic brogue, their Popery -
these "swarming droves" and "menacing degenerates"
"infecting health", and undermining stability
by "taking wages away from native labourers".

Ironic that History forgot
that these destitute Irish poor
were British citizens hi-jacked into penury
by the Act of Union:

and not Romanians, Albanians, Iranians,
Serbs, Slavs, Poles, Czechs,
not Bangladeshi Muslims,
not Hindi, not Sikh,
not Chinese cockle-pickers,
not Vietnamese gagging for air
in the backs of container wagons,
not sub-Saharan émigrés,
not Afghanis crossing the Channel in dinghies
and not Jews, et cetera

but itinerant beggars
that most of England
thought it wise to deny.

Words ...

Who will set down their narrative
these land-bound Irish poor denied the right of literacy,
forbidden their own schools by the Penal Code, their clerics
hunted down for sport, their look-outs on the priest-stones
gagged and bound, their tongues stopped from telling ...

Who will record their story ...

Their existence is as lists of figures, flat statistics,
mathematical calculations, emanating from across the sea
in Commission and Enquiry, Census and Report –
so that numbers and totals are more conspicuous than names;
size of tenancy more relevant than the tenant's identity;
amount of property more important than ownership;
medical records citing incidence, type and frequency of disease
(typhus, relapsing-fever, yellow-fever, flux, scurvy, dysentery)
more highly rated than patient names ...

Peel, Russell, Palmerston,
and the landed Anglo-Irish, like the Mahon family,
have their histories and biographies, even their mythologies ...

but who will name the names of these land-bound poor,
who will set down their narratives ...

"In the forty-five years since the Union no fewer than 114 Commissions and 61 Special Commissions were instructed to report on the state of Ireland ... Ireland was on the verge of starvation, her population rapidly increasing, three-quarters of her labourers unemployed, housing conditions appalling and the standard of living unbelievably low." Cecil Woodham-Smith, **The Great Hunger**, (1962), page 36

24

... and Pictures

In France, Gustave Courbet, feasting on Republicanism
and making more than a meal of historical perspective,
painted his angry challenge to bourgeois hypocrisy in vast canvases
ten feet by seven – to hang in his Paris Reality Pavilion:
swarthy-skinned French peasantry captured in majestic arrogance
as they made their way to market with their cattle – far cry
from the mythological gods and goddesses of the Salon school
with their shining silk-skinned limbs: middle-class France,
posed and posing in soft porn masquerading as Academy ...

In John Bull's England, since the Act of Union, the Irish poor –
their intimacies, misdemeanours, failures, happiness, their lives –
were lampooned and travestied by caricatures in *Punch* cartoon
after *Punch* cartoon: puny ruffians; scrounging rag-a-muffins;
deformed, out-of-proportion manikins pulled on colonial strings;
third-worldly-servile; gormless, formless, idiotic grinning, simian
things – no artistry charged to trace their being ...

Peel, Russell, Palmerston and the landed Anglo-Irish,
had life-size portraits to hang on the walls of stately halls ...
but for Ireland's evicted cottiers things were different:
when you've got no walls, knowing where to hang your painting's
really difficult ...

Fortunate, then, no Anglo-Irish Courbet
sought to draw their portraiture ...

*"Illustrations proved difficult to find. Perhaps because the years of the Great Hunger were a period of
economic pressure, paintings and drawings of contemporary events, with the exception of the wood-cuts
of the **Illustrated London News**, temporarily at least disappear."*
Cecil Woodham-Smith, ***The Great Hunger**, (1962), page 11*

"The national pet"

First report of inquiry into the condition of the poorer classes in Ireland, appendix F, page 385, House of Commons 1836

The old Irish swine,
high-backed, shimble-shanked, long-legged,
had huge, heavy ears
that flapped with a slapping sound
against thick pink skin
as it rattled about, feeding on table-scraps
inside the cottier's cabin.

Growing thin on lumpers
like its owners
was mostly bones, so slow to fatten -
then only managed low grade pork:
salted, and smoked over turf-fires,
the skin goldened by peat-smoke
for bacon.

Lived, like a dog, about the house,
bedding down by the low-lying cot
of leather straps and wooden laths
with mass of straw – the family platform-bed
for up to twelve, and always space
for vagrant strangers.

The kids' familiar, ghosting playtimes, outside;
and Paddy's pride: his right to drive
wending, delicately, with reed wand
and prodding to out-field fodder
in the mud-ruts, the churned earth.

Chomping through excess lumper stocks -
not just the rotten, rotting bits

but anything of a crop that couldn't be stored -
became efficient eating machine
with rich pyramids of stinking shit,
those coils of turd, rotted down to compost
(the higher the dunghill, the wealthier the peasant),
then spread over lazy-beds.

No wonder the sense of betrayal felt
selling it off to settle rent
or trading against oatmeal
in the lean summer months' run-up
to the potato crop.

Was the peasants' best friend,
excepting what both would devote
the most of their lives to:
the humble lumper spud.

"The Irishman loves his pig as the Arab loves his horse, with the difference that he sells it when it is fat enough to kill. Otherwise, he eats and sleeps with it, his children play with it, ride upon it, roll in the dirt with it."   Frederick Engels, **The Condition of the Working-Class in England**, *(1854), page 361*

Pyramid Economics

"Money is like muck, not good except it be spread."
          Francis Bacon, **Essays,** 15: <u>Of Sedition and Truth</u>

Whatever the name of the main ingredient -
          compost, crap, droppings, dung, excrement,
          faeces, manure, mire, muck, mulch, ordure,
          refuse, shit, shite, stools, turds, waste -
there's never any suggestion of wealth,
let alone something that anyone would desire,
or conspire to steal.

But the rundale-cottier – that idle, slovenly Paddy –
possessing no bonnets and boots,
          no made-up shoes, no eye-glasses,
          no scissors, mirrors, steel needles, combs,
          no clocks and watches, no patent medicines or soap,
          no steel tools beyond scythe, spade, sickle
              and peat-nicking loy
and   no surplus money
had dunghill-pyramids at his cabin door,
even piled inside, at times, beside his foraging pig –
such was their worth.

Stacking, turning, working, minding, mending
these mounds of stinking pig-shit, hay and root-waste
helped to measure his wealth:
their height (in quantity and quality of reek)
became stock component
for successful potato crops.

So lived all year with the stench of festering, smelling wealth –
the myriad citizenships (slugs, woodlice, maggots, beetles, worms),
the summer hum rising from its drying slime (imagine the flies),

and the sludge it would become under rain.
Pig, dung and spud:

with rent to be paid
that was a life-defining trinity:

pig, dung and spud.

"There is at present available two years' manure, not however twice the quantity of ordinary years, as
last year manure was not collected with as much industry as if the prospect of the potato crop had been
different."
Captain Edmund Wynne of Carrick-on-Shannon to the Poor Law Commissioners, April 25th, 1848

"The lazy-man's crop"

All it took: manpower   (Paddy had plenty)
       and women   (married young)
       and kids.   (plenty of these, too)

Cheap, as well.
No reason to reach deep into pockets
finding cash they hadn't got,
for sophisticated milling   (machinery they didn't need /
or expensive reaping tools.   didn't want)

Just a spade – and that, most likely,
passed down the generations,
so no forking-out.   (literally)

Land? Could be a problem.
Not ever owned – you bet -   (no overheads)
but loaned for labour, or rented,
though in high demand
what with the population explosion
and little mobility.   (save to the marriage-fields)

The solution? Divide, and sub-divide.
Even then, the earth worn-out to exhaustion
through absence of crop-rotation
and shortfall of manure.   (not everyone had dunghills)

Otherwise, the living was easy:
once Spring planting was done,
no extensive tending other than mounding
until the harvest-garnering.

In fact, not much to be done at all
apart from walking up and down   (a walkover, so they say)

and sitting, talking

almost south-sea idyll.   (Paradise Ireland)

Simple recipe for happiness:

man-power, spade, land

and seed-potato,
naturally.

"The little industry called for to rear the potato, and its prolific growth, leave the people to indolence and all kinds of vice, which habitual labour and a higher order of food would prevent."
Sir Randolph Routh, Chief Commissioner in charge of relief operations, to Charles Trevelyan, 1ˢᵗ April 1846, **Correspondence Explanatory of the measures adopted by Her Majesty's Government for the relief of distress arising from the failure of the potato crop in Ireland**, 1846 [735], page 139

II   Put that way – almost flippantly dismissive –
is to ridicule.

                  Better get down to facts.

First, the land: mostly flat and open; with little relief,
other than the odd thicket and copse, hedges and
walls counterpointing the contours' lift and fall,
and receding to horizons, blue in the mist, under cloud,
till the almost rise of the mountainsides
where horses with plough were cumbersome-useless
so couldn't successfully go – nor on hillsides –
or on the wetlands where place a foot and water
would rush bubbling upwards; and if, by chance,
land was dry, it was always the hardest of hard land,
the poorest, the stuff with stones that nobody owned.

Yet, given graft, planning, and a minimum of tools,
acres of land were drafted into the agricultural domain,
in vast nets of potato-beds raised between trenches
that drained the wettest of bogland; transformed hillsides
to terraces; and made nothings to plenty:

solutions so simple it's difficult to understand
why History so glibly diminished their success.

"Nor do I say it is filthy to eat potatoes. I do not ridicule the using of them ... What I laugh at is the idea of the use of them being a saving; of their going further than bread; of the cultivating of them in lieu of wheat adding to the human sustenance of a country ... As food for cattle, sheep or hogs, this is the worst of all the green and root crops ... I now dismiss the Potato with the hope that I shall never again have to write the word, or see the thing."   *William Cobbett*

III   Next, the planting: a three hundred year reminder
of farming's pioneering age, almost primitive
in its ritualistic rhythm of man, land and spade.

Starting in March, scrawing with grassauns
the packed-down haggard gardens and conacre land;
paring the sod-top; then, in May, raking away
the dry cover and firing to burnbate; and mixing
the ashes with lime/peat/furze – even sea-sand and weed –
and scattering this alternative manure (straw kept back
for thatch). Next, setting out the lazy-bed rigs
in six to nine feet spreads depending on land's wetness
with intervening trenches; then levelling the ground,
and sowing the lazy-rows, dibbing in with stiveens
the seed-crop (rose end and crown nose) or broadcasting sets
in line – stooping, placing, firming, and standing upright
again – then treading the length of the coarse grassland sod;
and earthing drills up with clods from
the dug furrow and when shoots forced through,
another mounding to push up bracts and flower mantles;
till dug up under the July broiling sun or westerly deluges,
soil treading between feet, mud hallmarking soles and toes,
and the piles of stony potatoes colding to the touch.
A week or so rest, then hacking the packed ground again
(more lunge and thud) for a six-week of second crop.
All this done waiting in hope, under the late summer rain.

"Potato ground was farmed with great care; spade cultivation produced deep ridges, and generous doses of lime, manure, and seasand – carried for great distances when necessary – nourished the seed. Consequently, yields per acre were high." Cormac O Grada, **The Great Irish Famine**,*(1989), page 17*

IV   The spade? Not ergonomically-designed like a Wilkinson:
all shiny blade, stainless-steel, rectangular, shaped and
sharp, and balanced against its light-weight alloy haft
in apple-green metallic patina;
                            but, where choice is matter
of beggary, just any old spade: the land-drain shovel;
the tudal; the clay-cutter; the round-edged, swan-necked
turfing-spade: all so many rough-hewn irregularities,
hammered by farriers in pitted thickness, ferrous-red,
with hafts, honed from oak or elm, made smooth by use –
no handle, but a two-handed pull on the wood, the ball
of the foot nudging the blade-edge till instep judded against
the spade's lug, pushing down: heavyweight mate,
a crude, semi-circular frowning scowl of a tool;
and everyone's need.

So, you'd be forgiven for thinking that all they knew
was lunge and thud – the suck and pull of bogland,
the splurge of mud, seep of wet. But, no – there was nicking,
too, and cutting those shaving papery-thin wafers of turf and
slices of loam; the neat pleats of edge;
the chipping delicacy; lifting rhythm; the arcing turn,
earth falling away; the crumbling pile; the grace of spade.

"*This root no matter how much you prepare it … cannot pass for an agreeable food, but it supplies a food
sufficiently abundant and sufficiently healthy for men who ask only to sustain themselves … peasants
and labourers.*"   *Denis Diderot,* **L'Encyclopedie,** *(1751-72)*

V   And the crop? After Raleigh's 1580s Cork plantation
        came a gallimaufry in type and variety: such as Rocks
        or "Protestants" imported from Scotland as Scotch Downs
        and Green Tops; Pink Eyes and Skerry Blues; Codders,
        Minions and Clusters (both Bucks and Bulls); Weavers and
        Thistlewhippers; Leathercoats; Kidneys (Red Nebs and
        Bangers); and those raised for sale to the wealthy,
        and used at table: the appetizing Apple and nutritious Cup,
        both commanding prices twenty percent higher than those
        grown for three million rural poor and first cropped
        as stock-fodder: the high-yielding, bland, coarse
        and water-holding, Horse or Lumper potato.

        So widespread the lazy-beds, and successful the crop
        that one third of the tilled land was devoted to Lumpers;
        and the peasants - the most wretched, but healthiest of
        Europe's poor – had their 14lb daily intake of potatoes
        containing almost twice the staple dose of iron, calcium
        and protein; and so vitamin-rich (both B and C)
        that pellagra and scurvy were scarcely found.

        Potatoes though were difficult to keep. So, pre-famine,
        other than next season's seedlings, were wintered in pits
        (even then festered) – the excess carted to markets –
        when unsold, tipped into ditches, or stacked-up
        in fence-gaps; or chopped and spread as lazy-bed
        top-dressing; buried; or heaped in fields and burned;
        or just turned, then left to rot – such actions spawning reasons
        amongst the Irish poor why God chose to blight them with
        hunger, famine, epidemic, and more.

*"This root … is tasteless and floury. It cannot pass for an agreeable food, but it supplies a food
sufficiently abundant and sufficiently healthy for men who ask only to sustain themselves."*
Denis Diderot, L'Encyclopedie (1751-52)

VI   And the folks: what of them? There, monumental
in their dignity, walking, bent beneath their loads,
and beneath the horizon-line as if they carried
the cargo of rain clouds pressing them down – there,
in the hard, stony earth of the wide fields
exposed, in turn, to sun, wind, and mostly rain,
their heads bowed, absorbed at their work –
bending, stooping, back-breaking work;
the torn calloused hands, aching limbs, grimed skins –
in a rootedness that tied them to the soil and gave them
their livelihood, and at their feet the ground
dropping away like the depths of a grave.

Or at table, sitting round the basket of boiled potatoes, eating
with fingers, peeling the jackets with thumbnails kept long
for the purpose, then dibbing the little bowl of salt and milk-
water garnish and mugs of buttermilk to hand. This done
daily, except for the "meal months" June to August when
potatoes were scarce, and the family pig sold to set against
oatmeal, grain, wheat. Even then, near starvation - because
for 2,385,000 folk no work other than those thirty weeks
of the year when potatoes were grown. These idiot poor.
These hard times. Such a life engendered a quietness: the
passive acceptance of hardship so ingrained that even
eviction couldn't erase – these peasant folk: the lazy-man,
with his lazy-beds, his lazy-row, lazy-crop … his family …
his spade …

"Such beautiful black eyes and hair, and such fine colours and teeth." Queen Victoria to King Leopold, 9th August 1849, in Eds A. C. Benson and Viscount Escher, **Letters of Queen Victoria: a Selection of Her Correspondence between the years 1837 and 1861** (1907), vol.2, page 111

The politics of husbandry: a footnote

Dr John Lindley, first Professor of Botany
at University College, London,
and Secretary of the Royal Horticultural Society,
regularly met with its vice-president, James Bateman,
concerning the latter's devotion to the orchids
which he cultivated in Knypersley Hall's fourteen hothouses
along with the grapes, figs, peaches,
nectarines, melons, oranges, lemons,
bananas, mangosteens, pineapples,
Malayan star-fruit, carambolas,
granadillas, kumquats and loquats
he grew for the delectation of his family and friends.

On less congenial days,
while Bateman busied himself losing a fortune
re-creating the world at Biddulph Grange,
Lindley was appointed by Peel's government
to discover the cause of the rot
affecting the Irish potato crop,
the repeated failure of which
was to reduce the population
of England's closest-to-home colony
by twenty-five percent.

Food for thought …

"*The potato murrain has unequivocally declared itself in Ireland… Where will Ireland be in the event of a universal potato rot?*"
Dr Lindley, Editor **Gardener's Chronicle and Horticultural Gazette**, 16th September 1845

The Potato Blight: *Phytophthora infestans*

Intrinsically pretty to the naked eye:
this minute, whitish fringe of growth
furring like down the leaf's contours;
and, under microscope, transforming
to ice-gardens with silent forest fronds
branching out - each long, thin filament
swaying and snaking, and each one tipped
with pear-shaped diadem creaming into pink –
like filmic backdrops for *The Snow Queen*.

You'd never guess this anaemic-seeming
innocence could unleash such devastation.
But in those pear-shaped crowns
are stored swarms of fungus spores
easing to be released by slightest of breezes,
or wafted to launch, airborne in drifting myriads,
or sloughed off by gentlest of dews,
to land – gradually - in thousands ...

More than anything, it's water that's important:
but then, not driving rains in raging gales –
they would drown out the downy-fringe.
No. Light rain is best. That, and warmth -
like those 1840s summers, muggy and moist,
in the West of Ireland –
that let the water-borne fungus germinate
and their zoospores infiltrate paling leaves

reducing juices, diminishing tissues
and discolouring to mortification

every frond, flower and stem
from green, through yellowy-brown, to black.

And no point chopping off infected top-growth:
no way would that delay or stop the rot:
for rain draining from leaf and haulm
causes falling spores to infuse tubers underground,
with black patches atlasing outer skins,
till the festering flesh within collapses
into palping masses of slushy pulp -

and the pall of decomposition-stink
hangs over the land.

"Ireland is threatened with a thing that is read of in history and in distant countries, but scarcely in our own land and time – a famine. Whole fields of the root have rotted in the ground, and many a family sees its sole provision for the year destroyed." **The Spectator**, 25th October 1845

Causalities

Had the blight fallen from the sky
    in rain so heavy
    that plants had become water-laden
    a "wet putrefaction" had set in,
    and the crop dropsy-rotted away?

Did it drop from the clouds
    formed by static electricity
    generated in the atmosphere
    by puffs of smoke and steam
    issuing from the popular locomotives
    newly in use in abundance?

Did it rise out of the ground
    from guano sea-fowl droppings
    used as manure;
    or spiralling as "mortiferous vapours"
    from "blind volcanoes" in the earth's interior?

Or perhaps it was the wrath of a Protestant God:
    visitation in the wake
    of the Catholic Emancipation Act (1829);
    punishment for the shame of a Queen
    counting the Nation's poor in the 1841 census;
    retribution against Peel's government
    for tripling the grant
    to Maynooth's Catholic seminary, County Kildare;
    a corrective to the Irish poor for
    their overbreeding
    their slovenliness and indolence
    their wastage of potatoes in years of plenty
    their reliance on the lazy-man's crop?

Or a fantastical happening
        like the Downpatrick fairies
        coming in the night
        and filching the potatoes away?

None of these
        but a "vampire fungus",
        seen in black spots of mould
        on leaf, stems, and undersides of plants
        which parasitically attacked root crops –
or so the Revd M.J. Berkley opined
in his *Observations, Botanical and Physiological,*
on the Potato Murrain, January 1846.

But was ridiculed to dismissal
by those who believing
        over-ripe cheese generates mites,
        bad meat creates blowflies
        and rags and cheese put in a box
        magicked into mice
the mould was formed during decomposition
as the result of fermentation and heat.

No wonder it took two generations and more
and further potato-crop failures
before the secret means of propagation
and the survival of blight were unearthed.

Official Remedies

The Scientific Commissioners' Advice concerning the Potato crop to the Farmers and Peasantry of Ireland – 70,000 copies were distributed by the Government to local agricultural committees and newspapers, with 30 copies going to each parish priest

- dry the potatoes in the sun
- mark out on the ground a space
  six feet wide and as long as you please
- dig a shallow trench two feet wide all round
- throw the mould upon the space
- then level it
- and cover it with a floor of turf sods set on their edges
- sift on this,
  packing stuff made by mixing
  a bowl of freshly burnt unslaked lime,
  broken into pieces as large as marbles,
  with two barrels of sand or earth
  or by mixing equal parts of burnt turf and dry sawdust

"If you do not understand this, ask your landlord or clergyman to explain its meaning."

Recipe for dealing with diseased potatoes

2nd and 3rd Reports of the Commissioners appointed by Government to enquire into the actual condition of the potato crop in Ireland, dated October 29th and November 3rd, 1845

- obtain a rasp or grater, a linen cloth, a hair sieve or cloth strainer, a pail or two for water, and a griddle
- rasp the bad potatoes, very finely, into one of the tubs
- wash the pulp
- strain
- repeat the process
- then dry the pulp on the griddle, over a slack fire
- extract the milky substance – starch – from the water used for the washing of the pulp
- mix the starch with the dried potato-pulp,
  peas-meal, bean-meal, oatmeal or flour
  to make good wholesome bread, pies, puddings
  and "farinaceous spoon meat"
- however, be obliged to note
  "starch is not the material which serves
  for the support of the human frame,
  and an animal fed merely on starch
  dies of starvation nearly, if not quite as soon,
  as if totally deprived of food"

"Perhaps you will not succeed very well at first but we are confident all true Irishmen will exert themselves."

Eradicating The Rot

"To eradicate the rot,
mix equal parts of oil of vitriol and manganese dioxide,
add to salt,
and apply to the diseased areas." *

From where would cottiers
living in rundales and clachans
get these ingredients?

How would the poor
drum up money for such expensive chemicals?

How wise was it to advise
this domestic manufacture of chlorine gas?

Though would later gain Government approval,
and with equally devastating consequences,
when visited on those unwitting sods
labouring to their suffocation
under palls of mustard gas
in the trenches and pits
of Flanders fields ...

(Social Darwinism apart,
  it's always the poor who're first to witness
  History repeating itself.)

* *Freeman's Journal, December 17th, 1845*

Indian buck

In France, they batten ganders down
with some paraphernalia of metal and leather,
so strapping each goose – solid, whole, still –
legs straddled, and feet trapped yet gangling mid-air,
the snake-head held high, beak forced gaping-up
with slicked tongue licking out, in, out –
orange against black – its gizzard visible
in the stretched neck's full length,
eyes swivelling in distress – and, there,
the basin-cum-tundish, regularly kept filled
with sun-bright corn-grits as brittle and glistening
as grave-chippings, in perpetual funnelings,
so swelling livers for *foie gras* …

And French hens, too: the corn-fed evidence
in plucked skin's buttery-sheen,
the jaundiced haunches, yellowing leg-meat,
force-fed plumpness …

But in Famine Ireland
force-feeding never entered Whig thinking:
for when demand for corn-meal grew, Lord Russell
ordered the closure of Poorhouse depots,
so battening the destitute down with hunger
evidenced in their swivelling distressed eyes,
starvation limbs,
visible gizzards,
the jaundice-yellow of relapsing fever,
livers swelling to collapsing,
the stink of dysentery,
the pang and pain
of passing the buck,
and passing the buck

The Leading Question

Not whether this is matter of Legality -
a question of who owns what -
so much taken when so little existed,
a plunder of sorts

Not a problem of Economics -
the issue of supply and demand -
satisfying the market,
selling at the best profit margin

Not Logistics - the trouble of transporting
so much, so far, through hostile crowds,
the need for armed guards, patrol boats,
the cost

Not Ethics - whose need is greater -
whether it's right to feed some folks
while others are consigned to death -
a question of choosing good or bad -
one set of lives over another

Not these, but the riddle
of where History ends and Literature begins

and whether any Poetry can be found
in this lading bill* for *Maiden City*
sailing from Dublin that first Famine winter

209 pigs	*24 bags oats*	*26 barrels of coarse meat*
5 calves	*43 bags wheat*	*11 pounds bacon*
7 sheep	*338 bags oatmeal*	*550 firkins butter*
28 pigs		*56 kegs butter*
		237 barrels butter

> *3 tierces lard*
> *83 boxes of eggs and butter*
> *1 hogshead ale*
> *47 bags potatoes*

Yes. Correctly read:
Poetry a-plenty:

> *47 bags potatoes*

exported that first Famine winter.

* Bills of Entry, Ireland to Liverpool, 20th December 1846, Merseyside Maritime Museum Archive

"I have called it an artificial famine: that is to say, it was a famine which desolated a rich and fertile island, that produced every year abundance and superabundance to sustain all her people and many more. The English, indeed, call the famine a "dispensation of Providence;" and ascribe it entirely to the blight on potatoes. But potatoes failed in like manner all over Europe; yet there was no famine save in Ireland. The British account of the matter, then, is first, a fraud - second, a blasphemy. The Almighty, indeed, sent the potato blight, but the English created the Famine ... A million and a half of men, women and children were carefully, prudently and peacefully slain by the English government. They died of hunger in the midst of abundance which their own hands created."

*John Mitchel, **The Last Conquest of Ireland (Perhaps)**, 1860*

Rich Pickings, Skibbereen 1846-47

"In … Skibbereen … the population lived so exclusively on the potato that no trade in any other description of food existed."
                              C Woodham-Smith, **The Great Hunger**, (1962), page 107

What scratting and scrimping that second summer of blight …

crowds following ploughs, or rooting feverishly
through lazy-bed rigs … men digging all day for things
as little as pebbles, then riddling through sieves …
taking the cold as stone back home, paring the rotting blight –
sticky-soft and collapsing through amber to caramel
to blackish palpy mess in its festering stench … picking any bit
with semblance of white and remnant of firmness … then grating,
holding firm amidst the slipperiness, and dunking in water
overnight, skimming the scum-doily, straining residues to mix
with oats for boxty bread …

and, exhausting that, homing in on turnips;
hungry women and kids gleaning fields like a flock of rooks,
scrambling after docked tops, devouring them on the spot,
mouths sliming with soil, or smuggling them home
to boil with oatmeal and mix into skoddy, or roasting
them slice after slice spliced between tongs over peat fires …

Land worn-out to nothingness, wayside and hedgerow
were next: stripping bramble and crab-apple, laurel and
holly berry; clearing stream and ditch of fish, frogs and cresses;
gleaning fields for leaf of dock, sorrel, dandelion, charlock;
worming in earth-dirt for pignut and fern root …
Till nothing …

All the time, the weather insinuating its further curse:
instead of benevolent westerlies bringing temperate rain,
a north-easterly crossing from Russia, gripping rivers to ice,

and trapping Ireland's length for months in iron cold –
folk exposed to snow, crusting frost, sleet, more snow –
six inches in early November - women and kids chilled
to shivering by nagging winds,
cheeks red-raw, lips sore, legs chapped, bare feet raw,
dragging across the land's frosted mantle their sacking blanket -
last thing unpawned in the 40,000 tickets
issued that Skibbereen winter ...

and these were the fortunate ones, working their fingers numb,
their brains numb on mindnumbing Public Works
for 8 pence a day ... better by far than the 100 bodies
gnawed by rats in December lanes and abandoned cabins –
and better than those forced to the workhouse,
900 cramming its 500 beds, and 197 deaths in just a month ...

With little planted, and less garnered, how could one expect
the twelve resident landlords to collect their £50,000 annual rent ...
and falling short of £15,000, Lord Carbery support the poor ...
not getting £10,000, Sir Wm Wrixon-Becher erect soup kitchens ...
not reaching £8,000, Revd Townsend do anything other than preach
...

Given this,
how reasonable to expect the Treasury to send extra food ...

Eating Solanums

Not *dulcamara,*
though its vulgar name, bittersweet,
might fit the bill:
this scrambling, head-and-shoulders highflier,
with its woody stem and bracts of flower:
paper-white surrounding yellow anthers
that push to cones – somehow foreign
like the Turkish turbans worn by tomato blooms.
        No, not this, with its pointed ovate leaves,
        their heart shapes and arrows;
        and not its jewels of berries –
        green, gold and blood-shiny red –
        that give, unhealthily, when you pinch.
        They could kill, if tasted in abundance
        so you can't eat these.

And not *nigrum,*
though there'd be relevance in the epithet –
the black nightshade –
drawing a close over things as it grows.
        No, not this middle-of-the-road climber:
        it's just shoulder-rubbing stuff
        with the same papery-white corollas,
        conical anthers, and oriental looks -
        not to mention its rhombic, lanceolate leaves,
        and those globose berries swelling to dullness,
        and black at that
        but which poison all the same,
        so you don't eat these.

Not *dulcamara* and not *nigrum;*
not bittersweet and not black nightshade
but *tuberosum*

which rarely reaches more than knee-height,
doesn't aspire, is somehow more containable,
lowly, homely.

And yet its stalk-haulms
angle into similar leaf-bracts, and – you guessed? -
stretch to florets of papery-white,
crowned by sulphur cones
with distinctly middle-eastern look
that slowly grow to berry-plums
as big as musket-balls, but green
and filled with next year's seed, not shot.

And, yes, they're poisonous too
so you wouldn't eat these, not these
but the tuberous stuff, lying underground –
firm, like colding stone: a treasure-plenty,
white and certain, and certainly nutritious –
you can gorge your fill on these.

Almost unthinkable, then,
that between 1845 and '50,
and not overseas in not-so-foreign England
but here, at home, in Ireland
millions were killed

not eating these
                the bittersweet
                the black nightshade
not eating these
                the lowly homegrown potato

                millions killed
not eating these.

Cooking Cabbages

Delia Smith's's **How To Cook, Book Two**, *(1999) page 121*

Naming them an *Absolute work of art*
and claiming *One medium-sized cabbage will serve four*
Delia confesses she's questioned for decades
how best to cook them:

whether it's the Round Cabbage ...

> (Impossible unwrapping its packed bandages
> to release one complete leaf squeaking
> as it unpeels, layer after layer, till surrendering
> its heart, bone-white and smooth. Tapped, it sounds
> hollow. Hard. Like a child's skull.)

or the pointed Spring ...

> (Young greens of thing. Discard those stripped-off
> floppy outers that hang, tired, like flapping skin
> of folks with malnutrition. Splice out their rib-thin
> stalks, white like clacking bones.
> Hear its heart squeal as it's ripped apart.)

the plusher, fuller Savoy ...

> (Its skin the furred skin of scurvy, rough and coarse
> as scabby sores; or acid-green like slimed tripes
> before bleaching, its meshy texture of dressed seam,
> or honeycomb. Read it like Braille. Slowly.
> It's a scrotal sack in the dark. Cut it. Feel it squeal.)

or the fatter January King ...

      (Bird's-eye of patchwork grass, veined by
       dry-stone lime-walls; or crepe of collapsed
      lungs under famine autopsy; skin leather-crinkled,
      and leaf-tips tinged with purpura as if bruised.
      Stroked, it's known to squeal. Sliced, it cries.)

Faced with large-scale hunger
would Delia be half so poetical,
or, cutting words, be satisfied
with squeaks, cries and squeals ...

n the Strokestown region during the Great Irish Famine"7,500 people were existing on boiled cabbage eaves once in forty-eight hours." **Roscommon Constabulary Report**, October 12th 1846

Dog's Dinner

On June 19th 1847, the frigate *Macedonian*,
captained by Commodore George Coleman de Kay
of distinguished service in the Argentinian Navy,
set sail from Brooklyn, New York: destination Ireland;
her cargo, 5,000 barrels of Indian corn-meal.

Forty-nine days' safe passage later,
she anchored at Cobh harbour, where was welcomed
from the Mayor's barge by Father Mathew;
and, afterwards, her full crew taken for pleasure-cruise
on the *Royal Alice*, with quadrille-sets danced on deck,
and the 1st Royal Dragoons playing *Yankee Doodle*
as they sailed past.

And, later that day, her officers were banqueted in Cork
with a dejeuner of
> turbot, salmon, lobster salads,
> spiced beef, rump of beef,
> veal, haunch of mutton, lamb,
> hares, tongues, pigeon pies,
> chicken, duckling, turkeys,
> sponge cakes, jellies, creams, ices, blancmanges, pies,
> tarts, cheese cakes, tartlets,
> grapes, apples, plums, cherries, strawberries,
> champagne, claret, port. *

Incredible to think, only six months earlier,
the *Cork Southern Reporter* for 23rd January 1847
had carried an account by one Dr Donovan of seeing

in a cabbage garden …
the bodies of Kate Barry and her two children
very lightly covered with earth,
the hands and legs of her large body entirely exposed,
the flesh completely eaten off by the dogs,
the skin and hair of the head
lying within a couple of yards of the skull …

No record exists of the Commodore's response
to the mismatch between his cargo's need
and his feast's bill of fare

though Dr Donovan felt compelled to remonstrate

I need make no comment on this, but ask,
Are we living in a portion of the United Kingdom?

*See Phyllis de Kay Wheelock, 'Commodore George de Kay and the Voyage of the **Macedonian** to Ireland', in **The American Neptune**, October 1953, page 256

Acts of Union

"Dependence on charity is not to be made an agreeable mode of life." Trevelyan to Routh, February 20th, 1846, **House of Commons, 1846** (735), Vol XXXVII, page 43

Not those of July 2nd and August 1st 1800
fostered by the Protestant Ascendancy,
whisked through English and Irish Parliaments
and engineered via the bribe
of 32 Irish peers in the House of Lords
         (Thomas Mahon's Strokestown baronetcy for one)
and the carrot of Catholic Emancipation,
dangling mid-air till 1829.

Not these Acts,
subsuming Dublin's Parliament within the Palace of Westminster,
and creating a united Protestant church
and customs union
(with – you guessed? – protectionist duty on British goods).

No, not these – they were never really popular
with 90% of Ireland's folk:

but the Acts instituting 130 workhouse Unions
recommended by English Poor Law Commissioner,
George Nicholls, after his six-week whistle-stop tour
of Ireland in 1836.

Immediate and truly inclusive these poor-law Unions,
with mock-Tudor-cum-Gothic facades
separating their planned 800 inmates into men, women and children
with families split between
cramped dormitories that lacked ventilation,
their beds, platforms of planks and straw mattresses
covered with rags,
the piss-tubs overflowing,
and cauldrons for stirabout and gruel,

meals eaten in silence off planks.

No-one imagined they'd be popular.

Yet James Tuke, Quaker relief-worker, noted

> *Hundreds were refused admission for want of room...*
> *In Swineford Union 367 persons died...*
> *In the adjoining Union, Ballina, 200 were admitted*
> *beyond the number it was built for.*
> *Hundreds were refused admission for want of room*
> *and 1,138 died in the workhouse...*
> *In another adjoining Union, Ballinasloe,*
> *254 inmates of the workhouse perished.*

"And this in a Christian country! –
This under the proud banner of British sway! –
This in a land united to England by a union
considered as sacred as a holy covenant." *

The Cork Examiner, January 6th 1847

Task Work

They gave them task work:
low hills to lower, meadows to level,
hollows to fill, rivers to dig deeper,
fallen walls to stand tall, fields to square off
and boundaries to build around acres
of grass-land walling nothing in but grass.

Gave them lines on their maps:
"meal roads" going nowhere,
tracks across mountain and bog
bringing nothing to no-one
and not meant to be travelled
so mostly unfinished, unusable if,
and built for thrupence per day with
two splats of stirabout's wetted maize
eaten off spades swiped twice on grass.

They gave them breaking of stone:
silver sweeps of hammers, the liftings
and falls with dull thuds like hollow barrels,
the slicings of light as splitting stone
into moon-halves, odd sparks glinting,
and rock splintering to chippings
for packing potholes in coach-roads:
tons done by hand, mothers and children
at penny-ha'pence a day, squatting
as knocking rock against rock.

Gave them shalings in baskets and creels
women reeling at barrow-wheeling
till abandoning stone-piles by roadsides,
their own funeral pyres.

They gave them task work: heavy and hard.
And grimmer still as winter fingered in
under bitter winds and snow, with hungrier folk
spraunged on haunches waiting for neighbours to fall
and pellagra, marasmus, starvation
staking their claim.

They gave them stone-walling
with never a reckoning
it might cost them their lives.

Gave them stone.

"The works should be unproductive so as to impose limits on the applications for employment-schemes."
C. E. Trevelyan, Memorandum of August 1st, 1846

Dubh Lough Tragedy: March 1849

I   At Louisbrough they gathered -
        this famine raddled six hundred
        of men, women and children - seeking
        food tickets and workhouse admission
        where, told that the Board Guardians
        were meeting next day twelve miles away
        beyond Dubh Lough at Delphi Lodge,
        were so exhausted for want of food,
        and darkness falling, they slept under
        hedges and scailps that bleak March night.

II   The next day, those remaining
        awoke to sun's anaemic disc, its warmth
        leached away by keening winds, to begin
        their rain-drenched, cold-sneeped trek
        alongside Dubh Lough's watery blade
        steel-eyed beneath March sleet, through
        the winding pass between Sheepy Hills'
        fieldscape and snow-capped Mweelrea mountain
        and, arriving at noon, found Guardians Hograve
        and Lecky eating a hearty lunch and not to be
        disturbed, so were made to wait outside, starving,
        freezing, well over an hour at Delphi Lodge.

        Hunger empties heads as well as bellies;
        reduces cravings to ravings; makes mad -
        but not these men and women, waiting
        with pleading eyes, their children keening,
        who, told there was nothing to be done
        but to return, set off back – broken, hopeless,
        exhausted - in freezing winds, cold rains,
        biting snow, a slow march of death besides
        this black finger of water, Dubh Lough.

III   And on the third day
        a burial party from Louisburgh workhouse
        under the Relief Officer's supervision
        set out for Dubh Lough

        where, because ground was spare, and soil thin,
        the bodies were dumped, without coffins,
        into a communal grave within a shallow pit
        then covered with thin layers of earth-dirt.

        So busy were they with survival
        no-one recorded
        how many of the six hundred had died.

"It is evident to all men that our foreign government is but a club for grave-diggers ... we are decimated not by the will of God but the will of the Whigs." *The Nation*, April 1st, 1848

Taxonomy of Famine Diseases

I   *Scurvy*

Cos dhub in Gaelic: black leg,
after the dark markings – crimson through to sloe –
of burst blood vessels blotching leg lengths
as high as mid-thigh, with great pain from inflamed joints.

Sometimes *purpura,* from the Latin for purple:
observed in spongy gums (touched, even gently, they bleed)
between mouth lesions, and contrasting angrily
with those whitish islands of ulcers
on gums, throat and tongue;

and in splotches of purpuric eruption – stinging, livid, sore -
on hands, face and chest.

Either way, bleeding from backsides:
haw-red, scarlet, carmine.

Colourful stuff, this.

II   *Bacillary Dysentery*

More colour:

the bloody flux: in Gaelic, *ruith fola*
sourced by bad food, and excrement traces on hands
and from faeces of flies;

diagnosed by galaxies on cabin floors
of blood-splats hardening from damson to scabby black;

but mostly invisible, hidden inside intestinal walls

where became inflamed in ulcerated honeycombs;

and witnessed, outwardly, by gradual marasmus
and the pain on faces while scowling
from bowel colic and rising drifts of gripe

till visible: the "looseness" –
liquid-thin mucous the rinsed-in-water colour of raw meat:
clear evidence internal gangrene had set in:

then shitting selves to non-existence.

III   *Famine Dropsy*

Hunger oedema, really:
dished out to those who had pawned every stitch
they reckoned would fetch a penny,
or had sold even the nothings they had, till left with rags
and were more than half-starved;

pillars of famine, were skeletal-thin to begin with:
skin dry as parchment and hanging in baggy folds
from skittle-pin fore-arms; shoulder-bones so jutting
that necks seemed hunkered into chests;
head and face skull-like; eyes sunk;

then slow swelling in lower extremities,
the onset of dysentery, fever, diarrhoea;
with anascara taking over:

limbs puffing up in girth
to triple normal size, fatter than fat,
and the body, blown up, bursting clothes,
swelling still, till waterlogged,
with lungs drowning in lack of breath.

IV   *Typhus, in several guises*

From the Greek *tuphos* (mist)
after the patients' clouded mental states,
their drunk-like stupor
in the later stages of the complaint;

in Gaelic, *fiabrhas dubh*: black fever:
seen in the dusky skin of congested faces
made to swell beyond recognition,
dark with burning fevers, and brownish down
on dry tongues;

otherwise, "malignant fever": with shivering deliriums,
lashing-out of limbs, raving and thrashing;
heads ready to burst with aching pain, vertigo,
ringing in ears;
eyes flooding with blood-traces; pulse racing;
sweating and unrelenting passing of urine;

and spotted – or "maculated" - fever
after the fifth-day dark-red rash attacking scratched skin,
and erupting in armpits, then painful redness
swelling around ears, over scalp, across cheeks,
through nostrils to larynx, then pharynx;

elsewhere, at extremes, "putrid fever":
whorls of sores wheeling legs and weeping to gangrene;
slime on limbs; festering stench:
loss of fingers, toes, feet;
with stinks so thick – ronk, rotten-green – they could be cut;

and "road fever": from vagrants who'd abandoned cabins,
or been turned adrift in filthy rags, so sleeping in ditches,
and carrying disease to soup kitchens

where infecting the town poor;
and as "Irish ague", same as that which plagued
Cromwell's Model army, paralysed by it in Ireland,
that bitter winter of 1649.

However named, conveyed one way:
by rickettsia in blood vessels of broken and bitten skin
infected with the faeces of the common louse of man.

V   *Relapsing Fever*

Named in Gaelic *fiabrhas buidhe*, yellow fever,
so framed when twinned with jaundice
and faces paled into straw, with whole bodies
glowing orangey-brown:
product of spirochaetes in fever-blood
and released into bloodstreams
by the common louse of man.

A sudden flushing running through limbs,
pulse pushed up to 150, and raging thirst:
but nothing kept down, so vigorous the sickness
and vomiting – retching at emptiness,
dry-heaving from deeps,
bringing up saliva-strands and vile bile;

pupils bulging to stupid looks,
irises inflamed sometimes declining to blindness,
and regular haemorrhaging
from nose, mouth, genitals, anus;
blood flowing richly till exhaustion;

then gastric fever lasting five days
and climaxing with rackings of pain
in every muscle, every vein; profuse sweating,

with urine wetting bedclothes.

But not ended yet.

Seven days later, a relapse.
And again. Again.
Even to a third or fourth session.
Death in evidence. Every time.

VI   Till just when you consider
it could be over
come the finishing touches:

for pure colour
there's nothing more fetching
than cholera.

"The total of those who died ... of famine diseases will never be known, but probably about ten times more died of disease than of starvation." C Woodham-Smith, **The Great Hunger**, *(1962), page 204*

The Big Issue

when does hunger become famine become starvation

when does disease become pestilence become plague

when does surplus become specialisation become want

when does class become exploitation become oppression

agricultural economy become improvement become eviction

when does *laissez faire* give way to genocide and holocaust

need give way to greed

migration to exodus

how

when

why

"*The land in Ireland is infinitely more peopled than anywhere else; and to give full effect to the natural resources of the country, a great part of the population should be swept from the soil.*"
Revd. Thomas Robert Malthus, **An Essay on the Principle of Population**, *5th edition, 1817*

Dan Byrne's Hunger

I *Free Meal*

This lazy-bed was long past raiding, the spuds gone rotten-soft,
their tell-tale stink keeping folks away for weeks, but that Friday
Michael, Patrick and Dan were magnetised by a riddling haze of flies,
their iridescent scarab-greens and wet-pebble blues, and that bizzing
niggling away at sanity like hunger pangs, till rising in clouds
when the lads arrived, arms thrashing widely and whooping at what
they'd found: a dead fox with curved black paws and ochre claws,
lying curled and bloodied like a stillborn child.

        Eyes dead and hard as glass,
his head was jarred against the body's rhythm, torso madly-angled
and framed in pain, with brown blood-streak slipping down
his snout from between the teeth's manic flash of grin, his hip
twisted where he'd struggled to free his right hind-leg from
the man-trap snagging at his shank's bronze-copper, the colour
already fading from his russet pelt, the blood smudging the vest
of his chest and his rust-red shoulder where he'd snapped and bitten
in his anguish, his flank draining to paler brown: all his burnished
majesty dished out between pain and death.

        It wasn't till Dan shifted him –
kicking first, then bending, and nudging gently, animal-like,
insistent, at the body's ironsides - that the foot-long spikes
designed to deter theft and spear feet were seen, now piercing
the fox's guts where he'd lashed angrily in his freedom-fight,
jagging first this way, then that. Retching at the writhe of maggots,
Patrick and Michael lifted him clear of the stakes, then tackled
the man-trap's spring.

        Today, for once, there would be no fighting.
The rituals of townland life insisted that this fox would be

wrestled free; every piece of him collected, kept safe,
and shared between the Reilly lads and Dan;
then taken home to folks beside themselves with relief
at this gift of food: the first meat they'd feasted on in weeks.

"Local tradition… still recalls fights over the bodies of foxes."
Roger McHugh, **The Famine in Irish Oral Tradition,** *(1956), page 402*

II   *Blood Let*

Was late March, around about five, the sun near setting,
when the Reilly brothers, Michael and Patrick, stood tall,
jars to hand, in Dan Byrne's yard, with their frisky stirk
spragged firm between them, spittle dribbling from its lips
and hanging on its amber coat - rough-plush and long –
horns just forming, pushing stumpy through.

The stirk's first time, it sensed the worst; could smell
spilt blood on the packed mud floor, so was restless –
smouldering and wanting to bolt, shouldering forwards
and back in a sort of reel-become-jig – the three lads shifting feet –
its stamping hooves, dust flying, head rising, then down again,
agate eyes rolling – wide, wild – snorting, and riffling,
and splaying its forelegs, lowering the whole of its body –
then tossing head back up again, triumphant, resisting -
breath caught, haloing, in the lamp's flickering.

Patrick stalling the stirk's struggling haunches against the wall,
and Michael cradling its anvil-head, Dad Byrne took a knife, and
dragged it against his thumb's run; turned it, glinting; whetted it;
then cleaned the blade on his sleeve. Dan readied the quart-jug,
and waited – held breathing - for the fall of that heavy quietness
before the slicing cut, nicking the snaking neck vein – blue-black -
the sudden head wrench – eyes writhing – Michael holding fast –
and quick spurts of rich blood, velvet-thick, till hot and gushing,
Dan nudging the jug to catch it – fresh blood-stars littering the yard
and glistening in the guttering light – all the time the stirk shifting
the rhythm of its being the length of its flank as, living its life-dance,
it tried defiantly to lift its head, stretching neck to bellow,
Michael hanging on. Worst was the stopping – always difficult
pushing that first pin across the incision, knitting skin together –
more bucking – the four of them soothing, and stroking,
till Patrick passed the strands cut from its tail

and Byrne plaited them, lapping, around the pin – the lowing
moans – its drum pulse - shivers rippling its frame –
all that surging weight being whispered down to stillness.

Wiping hands, Byrne racked the knife, then sloped indoors,
leaving behind the iron smell of blood – steam rising – as Dan
poured into jars for the Reillys to trophy back home, melting silently
through the night to their worry of starving kids, and Mary
to boil with milk, oats, cabbage stalk and herbs, then shape into
"relish cakes" for frying – and the hurt stirk put to the out-field
where the wound would grow whole again, till next time.

"A man… brought… cows to my father's father to draw blood for his starving family, about a quart from
ach cow." **Irish Folklore Commission, Cork Archive, Responses J**

III   *Lamb to the Slaughter*

Next December was when Dan confided his survival plan:
Lumper spuds rotting a second summer, the old pig sold,
stirk long gone, if we eat our meal, we'll have no rent …
Seen these sheep – way beyond the Mahon townlands,
in the south Roscommon hills… Being mountain sheep –
and wild – they're everyone's - have no bells
like those South Downers on Lord Westmeath's land – and no-one
sleeping out at night keeping watch. All ours for the taking …

*

Two days' journey later - ribbons of snow limning the hedgerows -
Michael and Dan lay low in the gorse, its unseasonal sulphur buds
smudging through dark green spikes, while Patrick singled out
this thistle-blinded ewe – *One eye is addled, be easy as breathing.*
The other two agreed – *We'll take her. Easy* - lean and battered
by wind, half-starved like them, scraggy beneath raggy coat,
with nothing but tufty moorland to crop.
For now, though, the waiting – December wind numbing bones -
blood thinning – hunger-pangs cramping – nearly out
of their right minds – kept going on promises of food …

*

Till nightfall: one of those thin winter skies – open, wide –
a full moon lying deep, almost hugging the horizon, then skimming
the tips of trees – skeletal - and slowly rolling, beginning to climb –
a buttery-colour, huge, haloed with rainbowing hues – and, beneath,
the spread of the hillside, ghostly-white close by, then slicing away
to grey, and black beyond – with a chill wintry wind that shivered
the eerie stillness – sheep barking between nibbles, and huddling
for shelter by shorn hawthorns, the stripped bramble thickets …

*

72

Moonlight gleaming in eye-beams – amber-red - meant they knew
the ewe's movements, though hadn't reckoned, sight blighted,
how keen her hearing, or fast her scampering, rattling through
blackthorns - zag-zigging through fingers and hands, Dan wrong-
footed on tussocks – slipping, sliding – ewe bleating and blorting –
frantic gambolling - back legs kicking, head bucking – making feints
- a stop, then panicky dashes at flat-out speeds – till Patrick had her
jammed fast between legs, left arm crooked around neck – a raised
right, and fall of his club – thump – again - and the ewe slumped
to her knees, rolled over, blorted, once, with red-black spilling
from nostrils and mouth ...

*

Beneath lamp, Michael did the skinning, slipping her greasy pelt
off like a glove – his knife slicing finely – the ewe's lean frame
pink as a baby, and nearly as thin – and the flat tombstone bloodying
to sacrificial altar. Trussing her crossed ankles with plaited straw,
Dan slung her over his shoulder, nodded *Go* and, nervous-laughing,
their hearts racing, eyes everywhere, they began their tramping
home ...

*

Years later, remembering this night - first of many saving them
from hunger, eviction, exile – they blessed those sheep:
All ours for the taking ...

"If the people are forced to consume their oats and other grain, where is the rent to come from?"
Captain Perceval, Westport Commissariat Officer, to Charles Edward Trevelyan, Head of the Treasury,
August 14th, 1846 (**Commissariat Correspondence I**, page 9)

IV   *Ground Work*

Coming home under September sunlight striping
through dawn clouds, Dan trawling his hedgerows
hoping a catch had been sprung in his rabbit-traps,
that the hemp he'd strung across the tell-tale runs
of flattened grass had snagged, and some buck
struggling his anguished freedom-dance had lashed
his last, the strawy-cord tautening around his neck.
But nothing. On nothing. For months. Though found
a grounded crow, its wings dragging the land fanlike –
so cricked its neck, folding beak over feathered breast,
and smudging the dribbling blood with spitty fingers
stuffed its still warm lump under cover of his shirt.

Was when remembered where the mushrooms grew –
stepping-stones pebbling the dewy field, their cream and
brown underskins feeling downy, stems like chalk,
their woody churchyard smell - so stuffed pocketsful.

Then tracking home, flanking Aughamore townland,
past widow Mairin's hut was where, coursing through
the early morning sunlight, saw white slice of raw onion –
half an orb - picking up the sun's shimmering, and
lying face down on the ground below her window.

Silence indoors. And out. No-one save him thereabout.
But left arm gesturing in opposite direction – just in
case – took a swipe with his right foot – then stooped
to scoop – its marble skin slipping, juice sluicing hands –
tucked in with the bird – sniffing fingers the rest of his day.

Showed surprise on hearing how Mairin had gone down
with fever – and dead in less than three weeks – seventy-one –
but never let on where his half-onion had come from.

"If the neighbours suspected there was any fever in the house, they used to steal up to the house at night time and put an onion on the window sill. They would split the onion in two. If the onion turned green they would know that there was fever in that particular house."
Recollection of Richard Delaney, from Cathal Poirtier, **Famine Echoes**, (Dublin, 1995), page 102

V   *Gone to Earth*

Dan still had his spade, Michael a stolen rope
and Patrick an abandoned net found while trouting
the Shannon, so it was all hopes that no-one else
had visited the earth before them.

Dan had calculated that by digging back to
the backdrop of rock, they'd eventually run out
of runs, tunnels, earthworks, and there'd be
nowhere for escape – *Is when we'll need
that net and rope of yours.*

But hadn't reckoned on the earth depth,
or that, once the top spade-lunge had shifted
soggy clods, the loam was packed that close
Dan could only slice and chip, so the dig became
more exhausting than he'd thought, and what with
the dug soil sliding back on where he'd worked,
and the fact famine rations had sapped his stamina,
before they knew it twilight was threatening,
making the dig a race against time.

Till, suddenly, the ground collapsed – a scrambling –
the lashing of paws – teeth needle-sharp and long –
and eye-patches flashing the face of a highway man
holding self to ransom – trying to back into the back
of itself – to shrink into its own shoulder-blades, but
attack at the same time – head thrashing - wild eyes
glaring – till thrown net – roping round, Michael taking
the strain – a snarling rattle – and it was all over in a flash –

spade raising for a single face-blade - thwack – steel against flesh – juddering – blood trickle – and a shuddering lump collapsing into the grey shawl of itself - yellowy claws stilled now, reduced to fork-tines and trapped beneath body weight - head lolloping oddly, the shape of a grey log, and just as lumpish – eyes glazed.

Pleased with themselves, they bundled up the sagging bag of flesh – *Quick lads* - before its living had been driven finally to earth, and death caressed its pelt with stiffness.

Theirs at last; one broken trophy:
that has-been of a badger.

'The next morning we ate… a slice of the flesh of fried badger."
M Doheny, **The Felon's Track, or History of the Attempted Outbreak in Ireland Embracing The Leading Events in the Irish Struggle from the Year 1843 to the Close of 1848** (*Dublin edition, 1914), page 260

VI   *To him who asks*

It was the smoke-plume and acrid-sweet sniff
of smouldering turf that told Dan the stoking-up
had begun, the makeshift chimney drawing him
just beyond Strokestown's fringe where the stone houses
melted into field edges. There it sat, squatting, ominous
mid-pasture: a hundred gallon boiler almost a carriage-girth,
taking four to maul it into place, the iron-red rust bleeding
through its bitumen black, and its clanging emptiness
dulled as it filled with a mix of water, oats, Indian buck,
onions, turnip, carrots, pease-meal and steeped ox-head
(its tongue long since promised to the Reverend Lloyd).

Loitering at the crowd edge, Dan marvelled where the rest
had magicked from – distant townlanders gathering in knots,
passive as sheep, rag-bags of folk with children wild-eyed
in their thinness – queuing, noggins and cans in hand,
to hear their name called, for bread and soup; and all the time
the officious gaze of Crown Agent Knox, roster in fist,
and the Reverend Lloyd and wife Eleanor smiling benignly.

Patrick McGuire, the carter, wasn't given to waiting, so
parting the crowd like some runaway bull, shoved his way
forward, till confronting Knox head on, demanded *Soup*.
And had it: splashed scalding in his face; spun on heel, and
bolted, hungry-still, cursing *God rot to Hell you English turners*.
The rest might have been stone, standing there, silently,
waiting in a resignation that made patience a misnomer,
yet came to life once poured their quart of watery prawpeen –
some, driven by hunger, scuttling away to cool their cans
under running springs, others fanning the thin liquid onto planks,
then, on all fours, lapping catlike through their blistered lips.

As for Dan, he'd learnt to manage his famine pangs, so hung
lagging back, knowing from what he'd been told over poteen
at driver Cox's shebeen that the best would rest on the pot's bottom –
and the finest, the screb-crust, left to be picked off, its crackly patches
scratching tongue, and fingers glistening with dribbled fat and spit.

Later Dan japed with the Reillys *Sure, 'tis written in the Scriptures:*
To him who asks will it be given – or so Carter McGuire knows!

VII   *Grasping the Nettle*

Putting Strokestown's tree-lined street behind them,
Dan and the Reilly lads, billhooks and flax-rag in hands,
struck out for St John's, the Mahon church, Dan averring –
Even a Proddy God will provide – though crossed himself
like the others, then took turn rolling over the graveyard wall,
to stay waiting, safe behind headstones, breath held in a mix
of suspicion-guilt become penance-confessional.

Not sure if Reverend Lloyd was out calling, they zag-tracked
the yew colonnade, and at woodpigeon-rattle through branches
tried vanishing into trees, burying themselves bolt up against
centuries of feathery leaf in bluish-black-green with shadows
lit by scarlet berries, hard and inviting. *Theys Lucifer's blood* –
Michael jibed, schooled with the other townland kids not to eat
by Father Geraghty - *Will whip you boys straight down to Hell.*

Once out into the clearing, their prize was sighted: regiments
of angular stems, nearly three feet tall, hanging with flags of leaves,
and dressed in tresses of yellowing seeds as gritty as last season's
salmon roe. *See whys we needed our flax-rag* – and Dan had a bunch
of strands tightly grasped in his left hand, while his right slashed in
arcs of light, the billhook slicing through wiry veins, leaving sap
weeping anaemically. The other two grinned at Dan's quipping –
There's nothing stopping us cropping the alls of them.

Twenty minutes of frantic hacking - frond-piles divided
equally - life draining out of teethed leaves curling under the sun.
Then all the time taking care to keep hands, arms, legs clear –
quick bandaging with flax - to carry home, feeling bolder now,
knowing cabins would clatter with the flash of knives on table
and bench, the leaves macerated to dark green seeps, then mixed
with soaked oats for stouping into week-long soup.

Patrick it was had the last words –
Better than starving, this stinging Proddys.
And with God's own weeds.

"I heard my own mother to say she saw the people travelling miles to the graveyards to gather the nettles... They grew higher and better in graveyards than any other where."
Irish Folklore Commission, Cork Archive, ii 10

VIII   *Famine Pit*

It was Dan's plan. He'd been told they were giving folk
one shilling each corpse, so since the family donkey
had long gone for food and its cart bartered, he'd
had to fall back to calling on the Reilly lads – Michael
and Pat – knowing, though, they wouldn't refuse:
their six-pennorth share for sure ensnaring them.

O'Connor it was who told Dan – *Padraig has gone* –
and before they knew it, they were wresting the plank
from the back of his dresser, and placing it on makeshift
bench, their mouths gagged with rag, holding their breaths
as they bent over his fever-wracked corpse, swagged
its sagging weightlessness like a sack of praties, swung it up,
and bumped it, laying straight, on the board. Dan wrapped
his plaited straw tight – *For the carrying* - round the ankles,
while Michael tied down the head, fined back almost to bone,
Patrick steadying the lamp's nervy rhythmic swinging.

And then the slow lurch and stumble to the church –
five miles – through the night, the three of them taking turns –
two shouldering, one either end, the third carrying lamp
and picking out the coffin-tracks till they reached St John's.

Scanlan and Gaughan, guarding the graveyard against
marauders, sent them down to where mounds of fresh-dug clay
defined the Famine pit. Turning the lamp so its beams pierced
the gloom of the twelve-foot deep trench, Dan scanned the tumbled
pile of bodies, and amid the mix of limbs and swollen forms
picked out the shape of six faces and heads. He blenched, then
retched at the rising stench.
                              Once more standing tall, he gave
the pre-agreed head-signal, and Michael and Patrick slipped off
the knotted straw, and angling the plank slid Padraig – *Amen Amen*

thudding down the hole's darkness to the giving squelch.

Feelings numbed and coffin-pence smarting in palms, they picked
their silent five miles back home. Once safe, they stored the plank
in Dan's roof. Was days later their shoulders lost their ache
and they recovered their tongues again.

'They dug graves 12 foot deep and put seven or eight bodies into each grave. They never put coffins on
them at all. Some of the bodies used to swell up and when they would be dropped in to the grave they
would burst."   John Doyle, Rasheenmore, **Irish Folklore Commission** 1075: 200

IX   *Sloe Progress*

Dan and his five Byrne siblings
like so many pavement ravens
had charted them throughout March
in claphatch and trackside: swags of white stars
lagging along hedgerows, their delicate five petals
stark against the dark thorns.

September was when, young Feargus dead,
the rest of bairns bone-thin, the Byrnes
returned, Dan hoping that chaffinches hadn't
filched the crop – *See, some there. Look There.*
And there – amidst sprigs of twig, and not yet
fully ripe: sloes, bluish-black and wrapped
in waxy must of greyish bloom.

Taken days before ready, else others
would plunder, they teethed into them,
there and then, cramming mouths with blackness –
whole fruit, hard and firm as pebbles –
that acrid seep from acid-yellow flesh,
till spilling to burst between jammed lips,
juice running glistening down chins,
onto licking fingers; two minutes' greedy eating;
spitting pips; the hard swallowing; the young ones
blarting, stomach griping with aches
of sudden fulness after conacre failures
and days without food.
Some relief. Hunger pangs numbed, aching sated,
then minds dulled by hedgerows' emptiness:
slow dawning that everyone's tomorrows
had been garnered hastily away.

"Children searched ... the bogs and mountains for berries."
                    Roger J McHugh, **Food During The Famine**, (1956), page 399

Almost an hour's loading that December morning,
lamps guttering in the chilling wind; the gangmaster
cracking whip; cows, bullocks - square Irish blacks -
barely visible through the dark apart from the beams
of light trapped by their amber eyes in the rhythmic
river-surge, heads, rumps, flanks rising and falling,
hooves clacking on gangplanks and skittering in shit,
cattle sashaying, all the time shoving and being shoved
into the steerage hold, steam and breath spiraling ...
While standing, passive, silent at Sligo dockside, nigh on
two hundred famine passengers waiting to board. And Dan
among them. How he'd landed here, he'd no idea,
but since the Reilly lads had been lost to fever, he'd been
anchorless. So drifted west. Thought it was Liverpool
not London he was heading for, so couldn't understand
why *Londonderry* was limed across the steamer's prow.
Once on board, all anticipation, underscored by the engine's
thrumming, the steamer slipping clear of Drumcliff Bay
with Sligo cupped in the inlet behind, the 8a.m. December sun,
thin and milky, casting pale angles between clouds and
bathing the sea in pewter light. Dan hadn't seen such vast
expanse of water, so the Shannon and Lough Ree dwindled into
insignificance against the tumbling Atlantic's grey-brown reach.
Behind him, huge slabs of rock as if they'd been lifted and
slapped down at all angles - Slieve League - some strata vertical,
others pulled as if the rock were slurry - the Cliffs of Bunglass -
like slices of cattle-hide, stretched, unrumpled. And Dan,
transfixed, humbled by the surge and boil of the Atlantic
where his and millions others' New Edens would begin.

*"At 8 a.m. on Friday 1 December 1848, the steamer **Londonderry** left Sligo for Liverpool with a cargo of
passengers and cattle... Two days later she arrived at Liverpool with 72 of her 174 passengers dead."*
Moving Here: **Migration Histories:** *www.movinghere.org.uk.* **Tragedy at Sea**
One of those passengers may have been Dan

Ballast

I   *Definitions*

Ballast: from M.E. bar "bare" (in this case "mere") + last "a load,
burden".

- (Naut) Any heavy substance, as stone, iron, etc. carried
  temporarily or permanently, in the hold to sink a vessel in the
  water to such a depth as to prevent capsizing.
- That which gives, or helps to maintain, uprightness, mental,
  moral, or political stability, steadiness, and security.
- *in ballast*, a ship carrying only ballast; carrying no cargo.

II   *Manifest*

The invoice from John Harrison of Galway
placed in the Tradesman's Bills for 1848
at the Quit Rent Office Papers, Dublin
for outfitting 261 emigrant tenants   *counted, not numbered*
evicted by the Crown from Ballykilcline
was £181 2s 10d expended on clothes   *who measured them?*

for	88 women	1 gown
		2 petticoats
		2 caps
		2 chemises
		1 shawl
	girls under 9	ditto, but without caps
	58 men	1 "Body coat"
		1 vest
		1 trousers of "Frize" (frieze)

boys 14-18   ditto, jacket replacing "Body coat"
boys up to 9   a Glengarry cap   44 in total
lads under 6   dresses   18 in total

a uniform of sorts
no striped pyjamas

and a £35 bill for shoes   140 pairs   *how arrive at sizing?*
plain brogues costing 5/-
to 7/- or 2 weeks wages
of male-workers

wearing which was a novelty
for folk hardened to going barefoot
through snow, or on flint, on stone,
on mud-rutted roads
and who, after pawning their nothings,
travelled in what rags they had left
carrying in hand their crossing-rations

salted fish, bran,
oat-cakes

and a strip of townland turf
treasured next to their skin

III   *Bills of Entry, Liverpool Customs House - 1848*

May 1ˢᵗ
Manifest for the *Erin* from Dublin
a never-before-seen entry:
12 bales Rags – approximately 4 tons of cloth -
from turf-smoked shawls, ragged pants and shifts
which, passing hands for food, had become bundled up
for pulping to parchment at English paper mills –

the stuff Poor Law Commission Reports
and Eviction Bills were printed on ...

July 3ʳᵈ
Another fresh entry:
from the manifest of Limerick's *Forget-Me-Not*:
26 bags of Hair for W Jackson & Son
destined for Liverpool's wigmakers and milliners
and culled from the clumsily-cropped heads,
the shaved and shorn crowns of "small girls ...
selling their hair to stay alive" * ...

Fashion after all has its uses, its excuses ...

Remember Treblinka:
bins of skin-slivers, tattooed for use in lampshades;
bones piled for soap; teeth pulled for gold; the spectacles;
tresses of cropped hair, for padding mattresses, filling pillows;
those shaved heads – six million – egg-like, imbecilic-grinning:
those empty vessels
going nowhere ...

* *Simon Schama, **A History of Britain 3**, (2002), page 227*

IV   *A weighty read*

"As movers and the moved both know, books are heavy freight, the weight of refrigerators and sofas broken up into cardboard boxes."
    John Updike, **Due Considerations: Essays and Criticisms**

Is it because   they were denied more than elementary education
                they could not read
                they had no books
these Irish poor
                were encouraged
                were pushed
                were forced   to move
their cabins scattered, burnt
their homes crowbarred, tumbled

and having none of anything

                refrigerators, sofas,
                cardboard, books

accepted themselves as ballast

89

V   *All Animals Are Equal*

In 1854, John Besnard,
Cork port's weigh-master,
informed a Parliamentary Enquiry
that he had seen a steamer setting sail
for Liverpool with some eleven hundred
emigrant deck passenger on board,
while stored below in the hold
were three hundred pigs.

Besnard's evidence mentioned
that despite travelling at half human fare,
the pigs met with better respect
because they have some value to someone.*

**Report From the Select Committee on the Passengers Act*, House of Commons, 1851 (632), Vol. XIX, J Besnard's Evidence, Nos. 658-6683.

Comparisons

The net amount spent
by the British Government
for relief of Famine
in its closest colony
was £7 million
or less than ½% of GNP
spread over 5 years.

Consider how this compares
with the £20 million compensation
to slave-owners at Abolition.

Or the £70 million
the Treasury fixed
between 1854 and 1856
for war in the Crimean ...

Comparisons, oh odious comparisons ...

Sentence Structure

"For he's the people's darling
Amongst the lot the only don
Who didn't take care of number one"

so sang the London crossing sweepers
when Viscount Palmerston resigned
as Whig Foreign Secretary in 1851,
a post he'd held for almost fifteen years.

What fostered his popularity were his vigour
and diplomatic swagger - not to mention
his jingoistic cynicism fringing on xenophobia:
fencing against France *"with a tenacity... like*
insanity"; suggesting *"Mehemet Ali... be chucked*
into the Nile"; and insisting Victoria shouldn't
"give the Shah the garter: he deserves the halter."[i]

This bluff drum-thumper of Britain's colonial power
it was who promised the Commons in 1841

> *as long as England shall be pre-eminent*
> *on the ocean of human affairs,*
> *there can be none whose fortunes shall be shipwrecked,*
> *there can be none whose conditions shall be so desperate*
> *that ... our moral support and our sympathy*
> *shall cheer them in their adversity.*[ii]

Six years later, when absentee landlord Palmerston
cheered his 2,000 Sligo cottiers with assisted passages
to Canada, the **Lord Ashburton** docking on October 30th
at Quebec was named *"a disgrace to the home authorities"*
with 147 of his tenants, *"almost naked"*, and 87 needing
charity clothing before disembarking; and when the brig,

92

Richard Watson, landed in November, the men *"riddled with disease"*, one of Palmerston's tenants *"completely naked, had to have a sheet wrapped round her before going ashore"*; while, the *Eliza Liddell* landing at St John's, New Brunswick in July brought only *"widows with young children, and aged, destitute, decrepit persons useless to the colony"*; and *Aeolus* docking in November *"with a numerous and distressed portion of his tenantry... unprovided with the common means of support, with broken-down constitutions and almost in a state of nudity"*[iii] quarantine officer Harding estimated ninety-nine percent of the Viscount's emigrants would remain a public charge.

Palmerston calmly shifted blame to land-agent Kincaid who explained

> *Large sums were expended in providing clothing ...*
> *but we suppose the hardships of a rough sea voyage*
> *were too much for the inferior kind of clothing*
> *to which the inhabitants of the west of Ireland are accustomed.*[iv]

No doubt "the people's darling" smiled at this demonstration of what he'd prescribed on a previous occasion:

> *Sentences should ... begin with the nominative,*
> *go on with the verb and end with the accusative.*[v]

i.   Greville, **Memoirs**, Part II, vol. II, page 82.

ii. House of Commons, 1841, [in H.C.F. Bell, **Lord Palmerston**, vol. I, page 232.]

iii. **Papers Relating to Emigration to British North America, 150**, House of Commons, 1847-48, (50), xlvii, page 157.

iv. **Journals of the Legislative Assembly of the Province of Canada**, Vol. 7, Appendix W.

v.   H.C. F. Bell, **Lord Palmerston**, vol. I, page 261.

Summing Up

George Charles Bingham was good with sums.

Born the year of the Act of Union,   1800
at age 26 had mastered the practice of addition
and by a series of calculations had arrived at
his formula for living: "Bingham's Dandies".
Being smart, added this to his Castlebar baronetcy.
Didn't challenge any theorems, despite going off
at a tangent – overseas in England – where became
absentee landlord, his estates leftover to land-agents,
the O'Malleys, who grappled with long divisions
of land, and the multiplications of tenant-families.

Further calculations, without showing his workings,
returned Bingham as Mayo's M.P. His method?
Polling votes from neighbour Major Fitzgerald's tenants: 1826
no proofs needed to test frequency of repeat patterns.

A decade later, retiring to his estates on army half-pay,
this pure maths genius put an acute angle on his accounts
and figuring the O'Malleys - lowest common denominators -
had excelled themselves in subtraction of rents,
reduced their function to the power of none.

To clear next decade's slate took up applied mathematics.
His simple solution to statistical problems: massive subtraction
of 2000 tenants from Ballinrobe parish, no other remainders   1847
and by unequal equation, putting nothing to nothing,
found the surplus recurring, and Castlebar Poorhouse overfull.

Yes, brilliant with figures, this George Charles Bingham;
his highest common factor, his title: Third Lord Lucan.

But then, number-crunching runs in the family:
brother-in-law, Lord Cardigan, having totted up
£30,000 (at contemporary value) for his commission as Colonel
managed in half an hour at Balaclava
to reduce without differentiation
673 men to 113 dead and 134 wounded,
then integrated the equation with the loss of 497 horses -
a result which flabbergasted the Nation.   1854

And, four generations on, the Seventh Earl,
graduating to a higher degree,   November, 1974
foxed his peers by solving the unsolvable:
how to take self away from self
and leave nothing behind ...

"George Charles Bingham ...was a professional soldier ... which is to say he knew and cared more about pretty uniforms than the management of men. By a series of purchases he became lieutenant-colonel commanding one of the smartest cavalry regiments in the British army, the 17th Lancers – 'Bingham's Dandies'." Robin Neillands, **Walking Through Ireland** (1993), page 77

Whereas

absentee landlords engaged architects
to plan vast mansions with Palladian gables,
sash windows, shutters, ballrooms and libraries,
and upper floors of bed-rooms

>cottiers, too-present-by-far,
>squatted in less than cottages –
>windowless cabins, slapped up
>from hedge-fence, sods of grass,
>and stone, and mud
>with a sack hung for a door

serving men made up huge fires
in massive Jacobean grates with decorated mantels
and baskets of logs garnered
from landowner's wooded estates

>peasants forbidden even fallen wood
>from copses or rotten tree-boles,
>huddled over turf-fires
>in smoke-filled huts,
>slept as many as twelve to a bed

hob-knobs sat down to ten-course dinners –
beef, venison, pheasant, lamb,
sorbets, tender fruits, glasshouse pineapples -
flushed down with claret and other fine wines

>tenants fed on potatoes at every meal,
>with salt and buttermilk, later replaced by
>boxty bread, water-whelps, sowans,
>flummery and cheerins,

and when these ran short
dead dogs, nettles, leather-belts,
rats, grass

huge estates were consolidated
into grazing pasture,
owned by handfuls of landlords,
their grounds pocked with follies
and gazebos, family shrines and sepulchres,
even their pets' resting places

millions died, landless,
buried in unmarked graves

"What was the condition of the people ... during the reign of the late Whig government? Your commerce
- did that thrive? Your manufactures – were they encouraged? Your fisheries – were they protected?
Your wastelands – they were two million acres – were they reclaimed? How fared the Irish artisan – how
fared the Irish peasant? Where one pined, as he pines yet, in your beggared cities, the other starved as he
yet starves, upon your fruitful soil."

Thomas Francis Meagher, June 1846

Close Textual Reading

Google the internet for themes, motifs and symbols
in Oscar Wilde's *The Importance of Being Earnest.*

Make jottings as follows:
>   an exposé of Victorian preoccupation
>   with respectability, social position and income
>   in which food and eating appear frequently
>   and are almost always sources of conflict
>> e.g. Algernon more worried about absence
>> of cucumber sandwiches (which he ate)
>> than serious issues of social class.

Note   action taking place against discussion
>   of constraints of morality;
>   hypocrisy and Victorian duplicity;
>   manners and sincerity;
>   lies and deceit;
>   several jokes about death.

Recall that famine poem Oscar's mother, Jane Elgee,
writing under the pseudonym of *Speranza*
placed in *The Nation* for January 23, 1847:

"Weary men what reap ye?" *Golden corn for the stranger.*
"What sow ye?" *Human corses which wait for the avenger.*
"Fainting forms, hunger-stricken, what see ye in the offing?"
Stately ships to bear our food away, amid the stranger's scoffing.
"There's a proud array of soldiers – what do they round your door?"
They guard our master's granaries from the thin hand of the poor.
"Pale mothers, wherefore weeping?" *Would to God that we were dead –*
Our children swoon before us and we cannot give them bread.

Reckon, given her pseudonym
(*Speranza* is Italian for hope, expectation and trust)
that son Oscar's earnest preoccupations
shouldn't come as much as a surprise ...

But then you already know
the sins of the mother
will be visited ...

Think Cropping ...

taking the luxurious growth, and holding its slipping
hanks, firmly, between fingers and thumb, slicing finely away
till ready for shaving, leaving behind blunt stubble and making
looks hard-headed, less-than-human, with crown cropped
and bruised, and skin nicked where knives/blades clipped
in amateurish acts of retribution ...

Think 1st century AD, the pagan Danish "Windeby" girl:
taken; stripped; blindfolded; her fair hair pared away
to a bristling smudge out-lining her skull-line; then drowned -
weight of birch-strips, weight of boulders holding her down
in the twenty inches of watery peat-bog that were to preserve her
for centuries: killed for adultery, and not yet fourteen ...

Think liberated Paris, World War II: not the mob, jostling
and jeering, pulling, tearing; not the signs hanging around necks –
Nazi Frau – of collaborating women for opening their legs
and their hearts to the "other side"; but their shaved heads –
stark, hard, accusing - in a blankness that made them savage,
animal, out-of-their-minds ...

Think that "other side": the liberation of Treblinka:
not avalanches of suitcases, address labels intact;
not shoe mountains – laces, buckles, buttons, bows;
not bins of skin-slivers, tattooed for use in lampshades;
not bones piled for soap; teeth pulled for gold; the spectacles;
but tresses of cropped hair, for padding mattresses, filling pillows;
those shaved heads – six million – egg-like, imbecilic-grinning:
empty vessels parading the betrayals of **Arbeit Macht Frei** ...

Think Ireland: Cromwell at Drogheda; Wexford; the Battle
of the Boyne; Vinegar Hill; and Easter, 1916; or, nearer still,
Ballymurphy; Bloody Sunday; and the rest of "the Troubles"
with bigger-than-life murals; balaclava-men, Kalashnikovs cocked
for reprisals; the tar-and-featherings of women chained to railings
for betraying family, faith and nation, their cropped heads
eloquent testimonies of revenge …

Then think Famine Ireland, winter 1846:
not retribution, but mother-prompted offerings
in betrayals of sorts: these clumsily-cropped heads, these shaved
and shorn crowns, these raised faces, and not yet fourteen:
think these "small girls… selling their hair to stay alive" * …

And think 1847, 1848: the trading in flesh; the cropping of bodies;
the rich pickings of *laissez faire*: taking the luxurious growth,
and holding …

Simon Schama, A History of Britain 3, (2002), page 227

Knowing Hunger

I'm starving she complains, which really means
she wants a snack to fill a gap. *A Mars. Or Twix.*
Kit Kat. Anything. And soon. Like crisps.

She can't begin to imagine that depth
of emptiness, so deep that bones feel
hollow, and the ache reaches deep in veins
till pain drains all feeling away in
sensation wastage that leaves mouths dry
with a dry-lime taste. That Big-Dipper hunger
plunge, and pain burning as it worms inside
intestines, bowel churning and seizing, squeezing
and turning, the rising gripe firing stomach's cavern
behind malnutrition's bulging rotundity. The nausea.
And eyes dead as stone. Full to vacancy with
pleading silences where vulnerability screams.

No more can she inhabit the mantle of these
than she can comprehend how her Dad's granddad –
after the double whammy of the Wall Street crash
and collapse of the Gold Standard – stood, cap in hand,
at the factory-gates, waiting to be jobbed out,
or blistered his fingers picking clinker and slack
from the slag-tips, bucketing-it up for his Mum.
For sure, his family knew hunger, despite those
sixpenny rabbits that lasted a week of stews
with turnips and swede. But even their pain
came nowhere near the starvation to be seen
in Strokestown's Irish Famine Museum.

And this girl, fed-up to the back teeth
with her Key Stage 4 History-trip,
her clip-board tick-list haphazardly filled in,
seeks refuge in confectionery.

No way could she face
a clutch of grubbed-up pignuts or stripped
oak leaves, nettle stems, shards of bark,
boiled roots of dandelion,

let alone the hunger pangs
eating out her belly, her chest, her arms, her legs,

her already empty mind.

Visual Aids

Flicking through Victorian issues
of the *Illustrated London News*,
these Catholic Paddies engraved as elongated shapes
with starved frames, triangular faces and eyes too wide
by far, and their young children, faces stunned
in a dulled gaze and prematurely old -
these rekindle images from inside the mind's inventory
that slow the progress of the turning page:

those archive films bearing grim witness
to Hitler's "Final Solution": Europe's Untermenschen
treading the tightrope of Lebensraum,
and brand-labelled by Stars of David, with sticks for limbs,
coathanger shoulders, baskets of ribs,
and eyes fixed on extinction;

or - hard on the heels of Darfur, Sudan, Malawi –
the newsreels of Africa's latest famine victims:
Niger's dispossessed children with old men faces
and no food for weeks - dysentery crusting down legs
and carbuncles of clustering flies around lips,
around eyes - their cow-like pleading eyes;

or just last week, trekking beyond the Nile-corniche
to Luxor's rutted muck and dust tracks that locate
the Nubian market: those starving Moslem women,
gracious in their leanness, their children so many
draped pietas across laps, their hands held begging out,
and eyes trying to find inroads into mine.

And now, cushioned back home in England,
my mind's revisited by these haunting images:

the remnants of what passed as Empire
reduced to humanity's ragbags, its underclass –
so much colonial fodder en route to genocide.

And, always plaguing me, those eyes,
those empty, questioning eyes.

"Each day – each hour - produces its own victims. Holocausts offered at the shrine of political economy. Famine and pestilence are sweeping away hundreds – but they have now no terrors for the poor people. Their only regret seems to be that they are not relieved from suffering and misery by some process more speedy and less painful." **The Cork Examiner**, *January 22nd, 1847*

Illuminations

My wife's monthly £20 direct debit
to Oxfam Famine Relief
doesn't really figure in the shape of things:

tonight, millions – their bellies empty,
and no idea where their next meal will come from –
will be sleeping rough:

starved   homeless   hungry

In fact, today's twenty quid is nothing
compared with Queen Victoria's £2,000 donation
in January 1847 to Baron Lionel de Rothschild's
British Association for the relief of extreme distress
in the remote parishes of Ireland and Scotland

let alone the £14,000 - at contemporary value -
raised from Irish soldiers in her service in India

or the $710 and sack of grain sent by
"the children of the forest, our red brethren
the Choctaw Indians" *

Not to mention the estimated £3,400
for window-dressing her colonial progress to Dublin
in August 1849:

        £2,500 on repairs to "dirty and dilapidated" Dublin Castle
        £500 for her reception pavilion "tent"
and   £400 on "illuminations"

Whatever light might have been shed - is shed -
when your belly's empty
nothing really figures
but food

See G Potter **To The Golden Door**, (1960), page 460
"It had been just 16 years since the Choctaw people ... had faced starvation ... It was an amazing gesture. By today's standards it might be a million dollars."
        Judy Allen, editor of **Bishinik**, the newspaper of the Choctaw Nation of Oklahoma

A Serious Undertaking

It's something of an unspoken joke
in our dwindling family that every time
we chance across our local undertaker –
usually at those before-funeral-moments
of sherries, broken-backed condolences,
shrinking selves into separateness, eyes
melting into tears, not daring one another's
faces – that he's sizing each one of us up,
marking us off on his mental tick-list of who's
his next £4,000.

> [Our kid-brother reckons
> being a funeral director "must be a gift of a job" –
> what with no hard sell, no bartering, fixed prices –
> just need regular practice in wringing hands,
> a liking for black suits, and a face that wears
> neither glare or scowl, but more of a vacant
> stare of manufactured sadness.]

How different an outlook from what John Mitchel,
the Irish radical, observed and published in *Nation*
for January 16th, 1847 - a piece whose punch-line
subsequently stunned his countrymen to silence:

> *They are dead! The strong man*
> *and the fair dark-eyed woman*
> *and the little ones,*
> *with their Gaelic accents that melted*
> *into music two years ago;*
> *they shrank and withered together*
> *until their voices dwindled to a rueful gibbering,*
> *and they hardly knew one another's faces;*
> *but their horrid eyes scowled at each other*
> *with a cannibal glare.*

Health and Safety Audit

Location: Isis Island Hotel, Aswan, Egypt
Remit: Lunch Menu, main course
                            Chicken / Fish / Beef   [again]
                            Vegetables – various, mixed
                            Rice / Pasta / Potatoes
Plus: Egyptian potatoes:
                            small, sliced, white,
                            ovate, in their skins
                            as if made for this plate.
Minus (overheard):   "You can't eat those skins –
                              they been in the ground!"
                            [for "ground" read dirt]

Time Span: Between meals, the Nubian waiter explains
                            he gets 200 Egyptian pounds per month.
                            [less than £1 sterling per day]

Risk Assessment: Suddenly, we're back in Famine Ireland –
                            widespread poverty, low rate of wages,
                            and, yes, plenty of dirt,
                            though different in mix:
                            more turf, and peat: less sand.

                            Major omission:
                            no chicken, no beef – little fish;
                            no vegetables, apart from charlock,
                            nettles, roots and wild berries (in season);
                            no pasta, no rice
                            and no sound potatoes, for several seasons.

Action: Drastic change needed.
                            To be ministered gradually.
                            Extensive collateral damage expected.

This Silence

is a silence of generations grown in the bones
a silence lying deep beneath skin
a silence that has leaked into the mind's blackness
that knows but cannot begin to understand

is the silence of survival in the mix of awed and awful wondering
and that shame of remaining alive while others suffered
piled dying in trench and ditch   heaped deep in pits
beneath skitterings of quick-lime   abandoned in any old hole
un-coffined beneath hedgerows   layered between wall-stone
                    the hundreds unknown
the thrown-away nameless generations without headstones

how could you begin to tell this to your children
to your children's children   how tell this

so has grown fat on scapegoats of denial
            wasn't our family   wasn't us   wasn't me

            not us   not there   we were not there

this not remembering   this cenotaph of forgetting

            has become our history

this silence   our voice

"There seems to be very little information or interest in the minds of the old people about that time [the Great Irish Famine]. Indeed, it seems there was a sort of conspiracy of silence on the part of their mothers and fathers about it all." **Irish Folklore Commission, 1945**

110

Acknowledgements

Thanks are due to the Editors of the following magazines and anthologies where versions of some of these poems formerly appeared: **Blood Line** (Blinking Eye); *Envoi*; *Iota*; **Poetry on the Lake:** *Wild*; *Quantum Leap*; **Poets Meets Politics Anthology**, 2017; **Sailing By** (Norwich Writers' Circle Competition Anthology, 2008); *Salopeot*; *Sarasvati*; *The Black Horse*; **The Wigtown Poetry Competition Anthology** (07/08); **Vision On** (Ver Poets Competition Anthology 2006); **Waiting** (Sefton Writing Competition Anthology 2007); **When The Tide Is Right** (Norwich Writers' Circle Competition Anthology, 2009).

The following poems have been awarded prizes and placings in (inter)national Open Poetry Competitions:

Free Meal	Commended, Ver Poets	2006
Blood Let	4th Prize, Poetry on the Lake,	2007
Summing Up	Commended, Blinking Eye	2007
To him who asks	2nd Prize, Sefton Open	2007
Ground Work	1st Prize, *Quantum Leap* 18th	2007
Famine Pit	Commended, Wigtown	2008
Journeying	3rd Prize, Slipstream	2008
Gone to Earth	3rd Prize, Bank Street Writers'	2008
Taxonomy	Commended, The McLellan Award	2008
Imagining Sow	3rd Prize, *The Black Horse* Poets	2008
Sloe Progress	Highly Commended, Segora	2008
Task Work	1st Prize, Sentinel Literary Quarterly June	2012
Dubh Lough	3rd Prize, Mungrisdale Open	2013
Indian Buck	Commended, Poets Meets Politics	2017

Cover painting, *'Where Now?'* by **Erica Brook**, (**www.ericabrookpainter.org.uk**) reproduced by kind permission of Jackie and Bob Foster.

THE HIGH WINDOW

The following collections are also available from our website, where
further information will be found:
https://thehighwindowpress.com/the-press/

Printed in Great Britain
by Amazon

57780129R00068